TOGETHER FOREVER

D1809432

The sun will always be shining
The sky will always be blue.
And butterflies will flutter by,
As long as I love you.

When I'm with you,

I don't care about the weather.
As long as I know,
That we're going to be together.

I want to hug you
For ever and ever...
And ever.

We may have our differences,
But there's NOTHING
We can't sort out,
If we love each other enough!

Love is like some plants.
If the roots are deep enough,
It goes on blooming forever.

Being with you is the nicest way
To spend every moment
Of every day!

My life is full of lovely things
But the loveliest of them all is you.

I've been flying high
Since you said
We're going to be
Together forever.

I never knew
I was only half a person
Until I met you.

Some flowers have yellow petals,
Others red or blue.
No matter what their colour is,
They all say, 'I love you.'

My heart is as light as a feather
Now we're going to be together.

How do I know I love you?
Let me tell you why.
It's because I want to be with you
While stars are in the sky.

I used to play
'Loves Me. Loves Me Not.'
But I don't need to
Now that I KNOW you love me.

I want to tell you something,
And say it with a rose.
We'll always be together,
Through life's highs and lows.

I want to paint the sky
With the words
'I LOVE YOU - FOREVER!'

I wished upon a star
That you would love me.
Thank you
For making that dream come true.

A rose to say I love you,
But what is this I see?
If it's what I think it is,
It means that you love me.

If love is like a garden,
Then lovers are its flowers.
And the times we are together
Are lifetime's cherished hours.

As life's journey passes,
And the years unfold
The years that we're together,
Will be the years of gold.

I've been living on clouds of joy
Since you said
Our love would last forever.

My heart is your heart,
Your heart is mine.
Now that we're together
Until the end of time.

I've brought you a flower to say,
'Sorry!'
- Sorry
That we didn't fall in love
Long before we did!

You turned all my wishes into Kisses
Thank you,
From the bottom of my heart.

I'm looking forward
To growing old with you,
Because it's going to keep me
Young forever!

I'll find a flower to give to you,
And give it with my heart.
For now that we're together,
We can never be apart.

When you picked a heart
To be with forever,
I was over the moon
When it was mine you chose.

One and one make two,
And being two is fun.
But now that we're together,
One and one is one.

Ever since you said
We'd be together
Forever,
I've had a spring in my step.

Now that we're together forever,
The sun will always be shining.

Every one of these petals
Tells me that you love me.
No wonder I'm smiling.

A gift for you to treasure,
Whenever we're apart.
Something only you can have,
The key to my heart.